• *Cooking for Today* •

VEGETARIAN MAIN MEALS

VEGETARIAN MAIN MEALS

KATHRYN HAWKINS

SMITHMARK

This edition published in 1996 by SMITHMARK Publishers,
a division of U.S. Media Holdings Inc.
16 East 32nd Street, New York, NY 10016.

SMITHMARK books are available for bulk purchase for sales promotion and premium use.
For details write or call the manager of special sales, SMITHMARK Publishers,
16 East 32nd Street, New York, NY 10016; (212) 532-6600.

Produced by Haldane Mason, London
for
Parragon Book Service Ltd
Unit 13–17
Avonbridge Trading Estate
Atlantic Road
Avonmouth
Bristol BS11 9QD

ISBN 0-7651-9861-4

Printed in Italy

10 9 8 7 6 5 4 3 2 1

Acknowledgements:
Art Direction: Ron Samuels
Editor: Vicky Hanson
Series Design: Pedro & Frances Prá-Lopez, Kingfisher Design, London
Page Design: Somewhere Creative
Photography & Styling: Patrick McLeavey
Home Economist: Kathryn Hawkins

Photographs on pages 6, 34, 48, 62 reproduced by permission of ZEFA Picture Library (UK) Ltd.
Photograph on page 20 reproduced by permission of Vicky Hanson.

Note:
Cup measurements in this book are for American cups. Tablespoons are assumed to be 15ml.
Unless otherwise stated, milk is assumed to be full-fat, eggs are AA extra large and pepper is freshly ground black pepper.

Contents

✤

CHAPTER ONE

Vegetable Dishes

egetables are at the very heart of a balanced vegetarian diet. They come in many shapes, sizes, colors, flavors, and textures. A shopping cart full of vegetables is going to be cheaper than one packed with meat and fish, so it can be more economical to be a vegetarian as well as being good for your health. Crisp, refreshing vegetables can help cleanse the body's digestive system and maintain the perfect working balance.

Don't just serve vegetables as accompaniments, make a meal of them: Coconut Vegetable Curry (see page 18) is packed full of cauliflower, okra, potato, and eggplant, and Root Croustades with Sunshine Bell Peppers (see page 8) is a combination of carrots, potatoes, celery root, and bell peppers.

Opposite: *There is such a large variety of fresh vegetables available today, a vegetarian diet need never be dull.*

STEP 3

STEP 4

STEP 5

STEP 6

ROOT CROUSTADES WITH SUNSHINE BELL PEPPERS

This colorful combination of grated root vegetables and mixed bell peppers would make a stunning impression on dinner-party guests.

SERVES 4

1 orange bell pepper
1 red bell pepper
1 yellow bell pepper
3 tbsp olive oil
2 tbsp red wine vinegar
1 tsp French mustard
1 tsp clear honey
salt and pepper
sprigs of fresh flat-leaf parsley to garnish
green vegetables to serve

CROUSTADES:
8 oz potatoes, grated coarsely
8 oz carrots, grated coarsely
12 oz celery root, grated
    coarsely
1 garlic clove, crushed
1 tbsp lemon juice
2 tbsp butter or margarine,
    melted
1 egg, beaten
1 tbsp vegetable oil

1 Place the bell peppers on a cookie sheet and bake in a preheated oven at 375°F for 35 minutes, turning after 20 minutes.

2 Cover with a dish cloth and leave to cool for 10 minutes.

3 Peel the skin from the cooked bell peppers; cut in half, and discard the seeds. Thinly slice the flesh into strips and place in a shallow dish.

4 Put the oil, vinegar, mustard, honey, and seasoning in a small screw-top jar and shake well to mix. Pour over the bell pepper strips, mix well, and leave to marinate for 2 hours.

5 To make the croustades, put the potatoes, carrots, and celery root in a mixing bowl and toss in the garlic and lemon juice.

6 Mix in the melted butter or margarine and the egg. Season well. Divide the mixture into 8 and pile onto 2 cookie sheets lined with baking parchment, forming each into a 4-in. round. Brush with oil.

7 Bake in a preheated oven at 425° for 30–35 minutes until crisp around the edge and golden. Carefully transfer to a warmed serving dish. Heat the bell peppers and marinade for 2–3 minutes until warmed through. Spoon the bell peppers over the croustades, garnish with parsley, and serve with green vegetables.

STEP 1

STEP 2

STEP 5

STEP 6

SPINACH ROULADE

A delicious savory roll, stuffed with Mozzarella cheese and broccoli. Serve as a main course or as an appetizer, in which case it would easily serve six people.

SERVES 4–6

1 lb small spinach leaves
2 tbsp water
4 eggs, separated
$\frac{1}{2}$ tsp ground nutmeg
salt and pepper
$1\frac{1}{4}$ cups sugocasa (see below) to serve

FILLING:
6 oz small broccoli flowerets
$\frac{1}{4}$ cup freshly grated Parmesan cheese
$1\frac{1}{2}$ cups grated Mozzarella cheese

1 Wash the spinach and pack, still wet, into a large saucepan. Add the water. Cover with a tight-fitting lid and cook over a high heat for 4–5 minutes until reduced and soft. Drain thoroughly, squeezing out excess water. Chop finely and pat dry with paper towels.

2 Mix the spinach with the egg yolks, seasoning, and nutmeg. Whip the egg whites until very frothy but not too stiff, and fold into the spinach mixture.

3 Grease and line a 13 x 9-in. jelly roll pan. Spread the mixture in the pan and smooth the top. Bake in a preheated oven at 425°F for 12–15 minutes until firm and golden.

4 Meanwhile, cook the broccoli in boiling water for 4–5 minutes until just tender. Drain and keep warm.

5 Sprinkle a sheet of baking parchment with Parmesan. Turn the cooked base onto the paper and peel away the lining paper. Sprinkle the base with Mozzarella and top with broccoli.

6 Hold one end of the paper and carefully roll up the spinach base like a jelly roll. Heat the sugocasa and spoon onto 4 warmed serving plates. Slice the roulade and place on top of the sugocasa.

SUGOCASA

Sugocasa is a tomato base for sauces. It usually contains pulped tomatoes, sugar, seasoning, and onion. If unavailable, use sieved tomatoes, creamed tomatoes, or canned chopped tomatoes; these will all require extra seasoning.

STEP 1

STEP 2

STEP 4

STEP 5

TEMPURA-STYLE BEAN CURD & VEGETABLES

Crispy coated vegetables and bean curd accompanied by a sweet, spicy dip give a real taste of the Orient in this Japanese-style dish.

SERVES 4

4 oz baby zucchini
4 oz baby carrots
4 oz baby corn
4 oz baby leeks
2 baby eggplant
8 oz bean curd
vegetable oil for deep-frying
julienne strips of carrot, ginger root, and
*   baby leek to garnish*
noodles to serve

BATTER:
2 egg yolks
1¼ cups water
2 cups all-purpose flour

DIPPING SAUCE:
5 tbsp mirin or dry sherry
5 tbsp Japanese soy sauce
2 tsp clear honey
1 garlic clove, crushed
1 tsp grated ginger root

1 Slice the zucchini and carrots in half lengthwise. Trim the corn. Trim the leeks at both ends. Quarter the eggplant.

2 Cut the bean curd into 1-in. cubes.

3 To make the batter, mix the egg yolks with the water. Sift in 1½ cups of the flour and beat with a balloo whisk to form a thick batter. Don't wor if there are any lumps. Heat the oil for deep-frying to 375°F or until a cube of bread browns in 30 seconds.

4 Place the remaining flour on a large plate and toss the vegetable and bean curd until lightly coated.

5 Dip the bean curd in the batter ar deep-fry for 2–3 minutes until lightly golden. Drain on paper towels a keep warm.

6 Dip the vegetables in the batter ar deep-fry a few at a time for 3–4 minutes until golden. Drain and place a warmed serving plate.

7 To make the dipping sauce, mix a the ingredients together. Serve with the vegetables and bean curd, accompanied with noodles and garnished with julienne strips of vegetables.

POTATO GNOCCHI WITH GARLIC & HERB SAUCE

These little potato dumplings are a traditional Italian appetizer but, served with a salad and bread, they make a substantial meal. If you want to serve them as an appetizer, they would serve six people.

STEP 2

STEP 3

STEP 4

STEP 5

RVES 4–6

potatoes, cut into ½-in. pieces
up butter or margarine
gg, beaten
cups all-purpose flour

UCE:
up olive oil
arlic cloves, chopped very finely
bsp chopped fresh oregano
bsp chopped fresh basil
and pepper

SERVE:
hly grated Parmesan cheese (optional)
ed salad
m Italian bread

Cook the potatoes in boiling salted water for about 10 minutes or until der. Drain well.

Press the hot potatoes through a strainer into a large bowl. Add 1 spoon of salt, the butter or margarine, , and 1¼ cups of the flour. Mix well to d together.

Turn onto a lightly floured surface and knead, gradually adding the remaining flour, until a smooth, soft, slightly sticky dough is formed.

4 Flour the hands and roll the dough into ¾-in. thick rolls. Cut into ½-in. pieces. Press the top of each one with the floured prongs of a fork and spread out on a floured dish cloth.

5 Bring a large saucepan of salted water to a simmer. Add the gnocchi and cook in batches for 2–3 minutes until they rise to the surface.

6 Remove with a perforated spoon and put in a warmed, greased serving dish. Cover and keep warm.

7 To make the sauce, put the oil, garlic, and seasoning in a saucepan and cook gently, stirring, for 3–4 minutes until the garlic is golden. Remove from the heat and stir in the herbs. Pour over the gnocchi and serve immediately, sprinkled with Parmesan, if liked, and accompanied by salad and warm Italian bread.

STEP 1

STEP 3

STEP 5

STEP 6

MUSHROOM & NUT CRUMBLE

A filling, tasty dish that is ideal for a warming family supper. The crunchy topping is flavored with three different types of nuts.

SERVES 6

12 oz open-cup mushrooms, sliced
12 oz chestnut mushrooms, sliced
1¾ cups Fresh Vegetable Stock (see page 76)
¼ cup butter or margarine
1 large onion, chopped finely
1 garlic clove, crushed
½ cup all-purpose flour
4 tbsp heavy cream
2 tbsp chopped fresh parsley
salt and pepper
fresh herbs to garnish

CRUMBLE TOPPING:
¾ cup medium oatmeal
¾ cup whole wheat all-purpose flour
¼ cup ground almonds
¼ cup finely chopped walnuts
½ cup finely chopped unsalted shelled pistachio nuts
1 tsp dried thyme
⅓ cup butter or margarine, softened
1 tbsp fennel seeds

1 Put the mushrooms and stock in a large saucepan, bring to a boil, cover, and simmer for 15 minutes until the mushrooms are tender. Drain, reserving the stock.

2 In another saucepan, melt the butter or margarine, and gently fry the onion and garlic for 2–3 minutes until just softened but not browned. Stir in the flour and cook for 1 minute.

3 Remove from the heat and gradually stir in the reserved mushroom stock. Return to the heat and cook, stirring, until thickened. Stir in the mushrooms, seasoning, cream, and parsley and spoon into a shallow ovenproof dish.

4 To make the topping, mix together the oatmeal, flour, nuts, thyme, and plenty of seasoning.

5 Using a fork, mix in the butter or margarine until the topping resembles coarse breadcrumbs.

6 Sprinkle the mixture over the mushrooms, sprinkle with fennel seeds, and bake in a preheated oven at 375°F, for 25–30 minutes until golden and crisp. Garnish with herbs and serve.

STEP 1

STEP 3

STEP 4

STEP 5

COCONUT VEGETABLE CURRY

*A mildly spiced but richly flavored Indian-style dish full
of different textures and flavors. Serve with naan bread to soak
up the tasty sauce.*

SERVES 6

1 large eggplant, cut into 1-in. cubes
2 tbsp salt
2 tbsp vegetable oil
2 garlic cloves, crushed
1 fresh green chili, deseeded and chopped
   finely
1 tsp grated ginger root
1 onion, finely chopped
2 tsp garam masala
8 cardamom pods
1 tsp ground turmeric
1 tbsp tomato paste
3 cups Fresh Vegetable Stock (see page 76)
1 tbsp lemon juice
8 oz potatoes, diced
8 oz small cauliflower flowerets
8 oz okra, trimmed
8 oz frozen peas
2/3 cup coconut milk
salt and pepper
flaked coconut to garnish
naan bread to serve

1 Layer the eggplant in a bowl,
sprinkling with salt as you go. Set
aside for 30 minutes.

2 Rinse well under running water to
remove all the salt. Drain and pat
dry with paper towels. Set aside.

3 Heat the oil in a large saucepan a
gently fry the garlic, chili, ginger,
onion, and spices for 4–5 minutes until
lightly browned.

4 Stir in the tomato paste, stock,
lemon juice, potatoes, and
cauliflower and mix well. Bring to a boi
cover, and simmer for 15 minutes.

5 Stir in the eggplant, okra, peas an
coconut milk. Adjust the
seasoning. Return to a boil and continu
to simmer, uncovered, for a further 10
minutes until tender. Discard the
cardamom pods.

6 Pile onto a warmed serving platte
garnish with flaked coconut, and
serve with naan bread.

CHAPTER TWO

Legumes

Legumes – beans, peas, and lentils – are the dried seeds of pod-bearing plants of the *Leguminosae* family and are also known as pulses. Rich in protein, iron, calcium, and B vitamins, they are highly nutritious, contain plenty of fiber, and are virtually fat-free. With the current emphasis on healthier eating, pulses are a must for the modern diet.

Pulses can be cooked in a variety of ways to produce economical and interesting dishes. Many of the world's oldest and most popular recipes are based on legumes, but here are some new versions to tempt you. Try them in burgers, such as Barbecue Bean Burgers (see page 32), as a Lentil Roast (see page 27) for an alternative Sunday lunch, or combined with nuts in Garbanzo Bean & Peanut Balls, served with a tasty Hot Chili Sauce (see page 22).

Opposite: *A wide selection of pulses on sale in a market in Oaxaca, Mexico. Beans feature in many of the national dishes of Mexico.*

STEP 2

STEP 3

STEP 4

STEP 5

GARBANZO BEAN & PEANUT BALLS WITH HOT CHILI SAUCE

These tasty, nutty morsels are delicious served with a fiery, tangy sauce that counteracts the richness of the peanuts.

SERVES 4

3 tbsp groundnut oil
1 onion, chopped finely
1 celery stalk, chopped
1 tsp dried mixed herbs
2 cups roasted unsalted peanuts, ground
1 cup canned garbanzo beans, drained and mashed
1 tsp yeast extract
1 cup fresh whole wheat breadcrumbs
1 egg yolk
¼ cup all-purpose flour
strips of fresh red chili to garnish

HOT CHILI SAUCE:
2 tsp groundnut oil
1 large red chili, deseeded and chopped finely
2 scallions, chopped finely
2 tbsp red wine vinegar
7½ oz can chopped tomatoes
2 tbsp tomato paste
2 tsp superfine sugar

TO SERVE:
rice
green salad

1 Heat 1 tablespoon of the oil in a skillet and gently fry the onion and celery for 3–4 minutes until softened but not browned.

2 Place all the other ingredients, except the remaining oil and the flour, in a mixing bowl and add the onion and celery. Mix well.

3 Divide the mixture into 12 portions and roll into small balls. Coat with the flour.

4 Heat the remaining oil in a skillet. Add the garbanzo bean balls and cook over a medium heat for 15 minutes, turning frequently, until cooked through and golden. Drain on paper towels.

5 Meanwhile, make the hot chili sauce. Heat the oil in a small skillet and gently fry the chili and scallions for 2–3 minutes. Stir in the remaining ingredients and season. Bring to a boil and simmer for 5 minutes. Serve the garbanzo bean and peanut balls with the hot chili sauce, rice, and a green salad.

STEP 3

STEP 4

STEP 5

STEP 5

KOFTA KEBABS WITH TABBOULEH

Traditionally, koftas are made from a spicy meat mixture, but this bean and wheat version, which is served with a Middle Eastern salad makes a tasty alternative.

SERVES 4

1 cup aduki beans
1 cup cracked wheat
scant 2 cups Fresh Vegetable Stock (see
   page 76)
3 tbsp olive oil
1 onion, chopped finely
2 garlic cloves, crushed
1 tsp ground coriander
1 tsp ground cumin
2 tbsp chopped fresh cilantro
3 eggs, beaten
1 cup dried whole wheat breadcrumbs
salt and pepper
fresh cilantro sprigs to garnish

TABBOULEH:
1 cup cracked wheat soaked in scant 2 cups
   boiling water for 15 minutes
2 tbsp lemon juice
1 tbsp olive oil
6 tbsp chopped fresh parsley
4 scallions, chopped finely
2 oz cucumber, chopped finely
3 tbsp chopped fresh mint
1 extra-large tomato, chopped finely

TO SERVE:
Tahini Cream (see page 78)
black olives
pitta bread

1 Cook the aduki beans in boiling water for 40 minutes until tender Drain, rinse, and leave to cool. Cook the cracked wheat in the stock for 10 minutes until the stock is absorbed. Set aside.

2 Heat 1 tablespoon of the oil in a skillet and fry the onion, garlic, an spices for 4–5 minutes.

3 Transfer to a bowl with the beans cilantro, seasoning, and eggs and mash with a potato masher or fork. Add the breadcrumbs and cracked wheat an stir well. Cover and chill for 1 hour, unt firm.

4 Combine the tabbouleh ingredients. Cover and chill.

5 With wet hands, mold the kofta mixture into 32 oval shapes. Pres onto skewers, brush with oil, and broil for 5–6 minutes until golden. Turn, re-brush, and cook for 5–6 minutes. Drain on paper towels. Garnish and ser with the tabbouleh, tahini cream, black olives, and pitta bread.

LENTIL ROAST

The perfect dish to serve for an alternative Sunday lunch. Roast vegetables make a succulent accompaniment.

STEP 1

RVES **6**

up split red lentils
ups Fresh Vegetable Stock (see page 76)
ay leaf
bsp butter or margarine, softened
bsp dried whole wheat breadcrumbs
ups grated semi-hard cheese
eek, chopped finely
z button mushrooms, chopped finely
2 cups fresh whole wheat breadcrumbs
bsp chopped fresh parsley
bsp lemon juice
ggs, beaten lightly
t and pepper
igs of fresh flat-leaf parsley to garnish
xed roast vegetables to serve

1 Put the lentils, stock, and bay leaf in a saucepan, bring to a boil, ver, and simmer gently for 15–20 nutes until all the liquid is absorbed d the lentils have softened. Discard the y leaf.

2 Meanwhile, base-line a 2-pound loaf pan with baking parchment. ease the pan with the butter or argarine and sprinkle with the dried eadcrumbs.

3 Stir the cheese, leek, mushrooms, fresh breadcrumbs, and parsley into the lentils.

4 Bind together with the lemon juice and eggs. Season well and spoon into the prepared loaf pan. Smooth the top and bake in a preheated oven at 375°F for 1 hour until golden.

5 Loosen the loaf with a spatula and turn onto a warmed serving plate. Garnish with parsley and serve sliced, with roast vegetables.

STEP 2

STEP 3

VARIATIONS

Chopped onion or scallions would make a suitable substitute for leek. Try using different herbs in the mixture to vary the flavor.

STEP 4

STEP 2

STEP 3

STEP 4

STEP 5

RED BEAN STEW & DUMPLINGS

There's nothing better on a cold day than a hearty dish topped with dumplings. This recipe is quick and easy to prepare and makes a nutritious one-pot meal.

SERVES 4

1 tbsp vegetable oil
1 red onion, sliced
2 celery stalks, chopped
3¹/₂ cups Fresh Vegetable Stock (see page 76)
8 oz carrots, diced
8 oz potatoes, diced
8 oz zucchini, diced
4 tomatoes, skinned and chopped
¹/₂ cup split red lentils
14-oz can kidney beans, rinsed and drained
1 tsp paprika
salt and pepper

DUMPLINGS:
1 cup all-purpose flour
¹/₂ tsp salt
2 tsp baking powder
1 tsp paprika
1 tsp dried mixed herbs
2 tbsp vegetable suet
7 tbsp water
sprigs of fresh flat-leaf parsley to garnish

1 Heat the oil in a flameproof casserole or a large saucepan and gently fry the onion and celery for 3–4 minutes until just softened.

2 Pour in the stock and stir in the carrots and potatoes. Bring to a boil, cover, and cook for 5 minutes.

3 Stir in the zucchini, tomatoes, lentils, kidney beans, paprika, and seasoning. Bring to a boil, cover, and cook for 5 minutes.

4 Meanwhile, make the dumplings. Sift the flour, salt, baking powder, and paprika into a bowl. Stir in the herb and suet. Bind together with the water form a soft dough. Divide into 8 portion and roll gently to form balls.

5 Uncover the stew, stir, then add th dumplings, pushing them slightly into the stew. Cover, reduce the heat so the stew simmers, and cook for a furthe 15 minutes until the dumplings have risen and are cooked through. Garnish with flat-leaf parsley and serve immediately.

STEP 1

STEP 2

STEP 3

STEP 4

MEXICAN CHILI CORN PIE

This bake of corn and kidney beans, flavored with chili and fresh cilantro, has an unusual topping of crispy cheese cornbread.

SERVES 4

1 tbsp corn oil
2 garlic cloves, crushed
1 red bell pepper, deseeded and diced
1 green bell pepper, deseeded and diced
1 celery stalk, diced
1 tsp hot chili powder
14-oz can chopped tomatoes
11-oz can corn, drained
7¹/₂-oz can kidney beans, drained and rinsed
2 tbsp chopped fresh cilantro
salt and pepper
sprigs of fresh cilantro to garnish
tomato and avocado salad to serve

TOPPING:
²/₃ cup cornmeal
1 tbsp all-purpose flour
¹/₂ tsp salt
2 tsp baking powder
1 egg, beaten
6 tbsp milk
1 tbsp corn oil
1 cup grated semi-hard cheese

1 Heat the oil in a large skillet and gently fry the garlic, bell peppers, and celery for 5–6 minutes until just softened.

2 Stir in the chili powder, tomatoes, corn, beans, and seasoning. Bring to a boil and simmer for 10 minutes. Stir in the cilantro and spoon into an ovenproof dish.

3 To make the topping, mix together the cornmeal, flour, salt, and baking powder. Make a well in the center, add the egg, milk, and oil, and beat until a smooth batter is formed.

4 Spoon over the bell pepper and corn mixture and sprinkle with the cheese. Bake in a preheated oven at 425°F for 25–30 minutes until golden and firm.

5 Garnish with cilantro sprigs and serve immediately with a tomato and avocado salad.

CORNMEAL

Cornmeal is made from corn. It is pale yellow in color and has a slightly gritty texture. It is available from healthfood stores, supermarkets, and delicatessens.

STEP 2

STEP 3

STEP 4

STEP 6

BARBECUE BEAN BURGERS

These tasty patties are ideal for a barbecue in the summer but they are
equally delicious cooked indoors at any time of year.

SERVES 6

¹/₃ cup aduki beans
¹/₃ cup black-eye peas
6 tbsp vegetable oil
1 large onion, chopped finely
1 tsp yeast extract
4 oz grated carrot
1¹/₂ cups fresh whole wheat breadcrumbs
2 tbsp whole wheat all-purpose flour
salt and pepper

BARBECUE SAUCE:
¹/₂ tsp chili powder
1 tsp celery salt
2 tbsp light muscovado sugar
2 tbsp red wine vinegar
2 tbsp vegetarian Worcestershire sauce
3 tbsp tomato paste
dash of Tabasco sauce

TO SERVE:
6 whole wheat baps, toasted
mixed green salad
jacket potato fries

1 Place the beans and peas in separate saucepans, cover with water, bring to a boil, cover, and simmer the aduki beans for 40 minutes and the black-eye peas for 50 minutes, until tender. Drain and rinse well.

2 Transfer to a mixing bowl and lightly mash together with a potato masher or fork. Set aside.

3 Heat 1 tablespoon of the oil in a skillet and gently fry the onion for 3–4 minutes until softened. Mix into the beans and peas with the yeast extract, grated carrot, breadcrumbs, and seasoning. Bind together well.

4 With wet hands, divide the mixture into 6 portions and form into burgers 3¹/₂ inches in diameter. Put the flour on a plate and use to coat the burgers.

5 Heat the remaining oil in a large skillet and cook the burgers for 3–4 minutes on each side, turning carefully, until golden and crisp. Drain on paper towels.

6 Meanwhile, make the sauce. Mix all the ingredients together until well blended. Put the burgers in the toasted baps and serve with a mixed green salad, jacket potato fries, and a spoonful of the barbecue sauce.

CHAPTER THREE

Pasta

Pasta is one of the most popular foods on sale today. It is available in a wide variety of colors and flavors, shapes and sizes, and can be bought fresh or dried. Whole wheat pastas have a chewier texture and are valuable for the additional fiber they contain.

All types of pasta are quick to cook and provide a good basic food that can be dressed up in all kinds of ways. From family favorites such as Three-Cheese Macaroni Bake (see page 46) to quick supper dishes such as Mediterranean Spaghetti (see page 38), pasta combines very well with vegetables, herbs, nuts, and cheeses, to provide scores of interesting and tasty meals.

Opposite: Simple, fresh ingredients, such as well flavored ripe tomatoes, are all that's needed to make a delicious sauce for pasta.

STEP 1

STEP 3

STEP 5

STEP 6

ZUCCHINI & EGGPLANT LASAGNE

This rich, baked pasta dish is packed full of vegetables, tomatoes, and Italian Mozzarella cheese.

SERVES 6

2 lb eggplant
4 tbsp salt
8 tbsp olive oil
2 tbsp garlic and herb butter or margarine
1 lb zucchini, sliced
2 cups grated Mozzarella cheese
2½ cups strained tomatoes
6 sheets pre-cooked green lasagne
2½ cups Béchamel Sauce (see page 77)
½ cup freshly grated Parmesan cheese
1 tsp dried oregano
black pepper

1 Thinly slice the eggplant. Layer the slices in a bowl, sprinkling with the salt as you go. Set aside for 30 minutes. Rinse well in cold water and pat dry with paper towels.

2 Heat 4 tablespoons of the oil in a large skillet until very hot and gently fry half the eggplant slices for 6–7 minutes until lightly golden all over. Drain on paper towels. Repeat with the remaining eggplant slices and oil.

3 Melt the garlic and herb butter or margarine in the skillet and fry the zucchini for 5–6 minutes until golden. Drain on paper towels.

4 Place half the eggplant and zucchini slices in a large ovenproof dish. Season with pepper and sprinkle over half the Mozzarella. Spoon over half the sieved tomatoes and top with 3 sheets of lasagne.

5 Arrange the remaining eggplant and zucchini slices on top. Season with pepper and top with the remaining Mozzarella and strained tomatoes, and another layer of lasagne.

6 Spoon over the béchamel sauce and top with Parmesan and oregano. Put on a cookie sheet and bake in a preheated oven at 425°F for 30–35 minutes until golden. Serve.

STRAINED TOMATOES

Passata is the Italian name for strained tomatoes. It makes an excellent base for sauces, and is available from super-markets, and specialist stores, usually in jars or cartons.

STEP 1

STEP 2

STEP 3

STEP 4

MEDITERRANEAN SPAGHETTI

*Delicious Mediterranean vegetables, cooked in a rich tomato sauce,
make an ideal topping for nutty whole wheat pasta.*

SERVES 4

*2 tbsp olive oil
1 large red onion, chopped
2 garlic cloves, crushed
1 tbsp lemon juice
4 baby eggplant, quartered
2¹/₂ cups strained tomatoes
2 tsp superfine sugar
2 tbsp tomato paste
14 oz can artichoke hearts, drained and
    halved
³/₄ cup pitted black olives
12 oz whole wheat dried spaghetti
salt and pepper
sprigs of fresh basil to garnish
olive bread to serve*

1 Heat 1 tablespoon of the oil in a
large skillet and gently fry the
onion, garlic, lemon juice, and
eggplant for 4–5 minutes until lightly
browned.

2 Pour in the strained tomatoes,
season, and add the sugar and
tomato paste. Bring to a boil, reduce the
heat, and simmer for 20 minutes.

3 Gently stir in the artichoke hearts
and olives and cook for 5 minutes.

4 Meanwhile, bring a large saucepan
of lightly salted water to a boil and
cook the spaghetti for 7–8 minutes until
just tender. Drain well, toss in the
remaining olive oil, and season.

5 Pile into a warmed serving bowl
and top with the vegetable sauce.
Garnish with basil sprigs and serve with
olive bread.

SPAGHETTI

Whole wheat spaghetti adds extra flavor
to this dish but you can use plain
spaghetti if you prefer. You may need to
adjust the cooking time, however, so
check the packet.

When cooking pasta, always time it
from the moment the water returns to a
rolling boil.

STEP 1

STEP 2

STEP 4

STEP 6

SPRING VEGETABLE & BEAN CURD FUSILLI

This is a simple, clean-tasting dish of green vegetables, bean curd, and pasta, lightly tossed in olive oil.

SERVES 4

8 oz asparagus
4 oz snow peas
8 oz green beans
1 leek
8 oz shelled small fava beans
10 oz dried fusilli
2 tbsp olive oil
2 tbsp butter or margarine
1 garlic clove, crushed
8 oz bean curd, cut into 1-in. cubes
1/3 cup pitted green olives in brine, drained
salt and pepper
freshly grated Parmesan cheese to serve
  (optional)

1 Cut the asparagus into 2-in. lengths. Finely slice the snow peas diagonally and slice the green beans into 1-in. pieces. Finely slice the leek.

2 Bring a large saucepan of water to a boil and add the asparagus, green beans, and fava beans. Bring back to a boil and cook for 4 minutes until just tender. Drain well and rinse in cold water. Set aside.

3 Bring a large saucepan of lightly salted water to a boil and cook the fusilli for 8–9 minutes until just tender.

Drain well. Toss in 1 tablespoon of the and season well.

4 Meanwhile, in a wok or large skillet, heat the remaining oil and the butter or margarine and gently fry the leek, garlic, and bean curd for 1–2 minutes until the vegetables have just softened.

5 Stir in the snow peas and cook for further minute.

6 Add the boiled vegetables and olives to the wok or skillet and he through for 1 minute. Carefully stir in the pasta and seasoning. Cook for 1 minute and pile into a warmed serving dish. Serve sprinkled with Parmesan cheese, if liked.

WOK

A wok is very handy for amalgamating pasta and sauces as it allows plenty of room for tossing the ingredients.

STEP 1

STEP 2

STEP 3

STEP 4

TRICOLOR TIMBALLINI

An unusual way of serving pasta, these cheesy molds are excellent served with a crunchy salad for a light lunch.

SERVES 4

1 tbsp butter or margarine, softened
½ cup dried white breadcrumbs
6 oz tricolor spaghetti
1¼ cups Béchamel Sauce (see page 77)
1 egg yolk
1 cup grated Swiss cheese
salt and pepper
fresh flat-leaf parsley leaves to garnish

SAUCE:
2 tsp olive oil
1 onion, chopped finely
1 bay leaf
⅔ cup dry white wine
⅔ cup creamed tomatoes
1 tbsp tomato paste

1 Grease 4 × ¾-cup molds or ramekins with the butter or margarine. Evenly coat the insides with half the breadcrumbs.

2 Break the spaghetti into 2-in. lengths. Bring a saucepan of lightly salted water to a boil and cook the spaghetti for 5–6 minutes until it is just tender. Drain well and put in a bowl.

3 Mix the béchamel sauce, egg yolk, cheese, and seasoning into the cooked pasta and pack into the molds.

4 Sprinkle with the remaining breadcrumbs and put on a cookie sheet. Bake in a preheated oven at 425° for 20 minutes until golden. Leave to stand for 10 minutes.

5 Meanwhile, make the sauce. Heat the oil in a saucepan and gently fry the onion and bay leaf for 2–3 minutes until just softened.

6 Stir in the wine, tomatoes, tomato paste, and seasoning. Bring to a boil and simmer for 20 minutes until thickened. Discard the bay leaf.

7 Run a spatula around the inside of the molds or ramekins. Turn onto serving plates, garnish, and serve with the tomato sauce.

QUICK SAUCE

For an extra quick sauce, heat 1¼ cups sugocasa (see page 10) with ½ teaspoon mixed dried herbs.

GREEN GARLIC TAGLIATELLE

*A rich pasta dish for garlic lovers everywhere. It's quick and easy
to prepare and full of flavor.*

STEP 1

RVES 4

bsp walnut oil
unch scallions, sliced
arlic cloves, sliced thinly
z mushrooms, sliced
fresh green and white tagliatelle
z frozen chopped leaf spinach, thawed and
rained
cup full-fat soft cheese with garlic and
erbs
bsp light cream
cup chopped, unsalted pistachio nuts
bsp shredded fresh basil
and pepper
igs of fresh basil to garnish
lian bread to serve

Gently heat the oil in a wok or
skillet and fry the scallions and
lic for 1 minute until just softened.
d the mushrooms, stir well, cover, and
k gently for 5 minutes until softened.

Meanwhile, bring a large saucepan
of lightly salted water to a boil and
k the pasta for 3–5 minutes until just
der. Drain well and return to the
cepan.

Add the spinach to the mushrooms
and heat through for 1–2 minutes.
d the cheese and allow to melt slightly.

Stir in the cream and continue to heat
without allowing to boil.

4 Pour over the pasta, season, and
mix well. Heat gently, stirring, for
2–3 minutes.

5 Pile into a warmed serving bowl
and sprinkle over the pistachio
nuts and shredded basil. Garnish with
basil sprigs and serve with Italian bread.

STEP 2

NUT OILS

Choose any nut oil for this recipe, but
remember to keep the heat low as they
are much more delicate than other oils.

STEP 3

LIGHTER VERSION

For a lighter version, use a low-fat soft
cheese with garlic and herbs, and low-fat
natural fromage frais instead of cream;
remember to keep the heat low or the
fromage frais will separate.

STEP 4

STEP 1

STEP 2

STEP 3

STEP 4

THREE-CHEESE MACARONI BAKE

Based on a traditional family favorite, this pasta bake has plenty of flavor. Serve with a crisp salad for a quick, tasty supper.

SERVES 4

2¹/₂ *cups Béchamel Sauce (see page 77)*
2 *cups macaroni*
1 *egg, beaten*
1 *cup grated sharp semi-hard cheese*
1 *tbsp wholegrain mustard*
2 *tbsp chopped fresh chives*
4 *tomatoes, sliced*
1 *cup grated semi-hard red cheese*
¹/₂ *cup grated semi-hard cheese with chives*
2 *tbsp sunflower seeds*
salt and pepper
fresh chives to garnish

1 Make the béchamel sauce, put into a bowl, and cover with plastic wrap to prevent a skin forming. Set aside.

2 Bring a saucepan of lightly salted water to a boil and cook the macaroni for 8–10 minutes until just tender. Drain well and place in an ovenproof dish.

3 Stir the egg, sharp semi-hard cheese, mustard, chives, and seasoning into the béchamel sauce and spoon over the macaroni, making sure it is well covered. Top with a layer of sliced tomatoes.

4 Sprinkle over the red cheese, the cheese with chives, and sunflower seeds. Put on a cookie sheet and bake in preheated oven at 375°F for 25–30 minutes until bubbling and golden. Garnish with chives and serve immediately.

THREE CHEESES

This recipe would work just as well with almost any combination of cheeses, so experiment with whatever is available.

An extensive range of semi-hard cheeses made with onions, chives, or other herbs is widely available. Other interesting variations include apple smoked cheese and cheese made with red wine incorporated at the curd stage.

CHAPTER FOUR

Grains & Cereals

The seeds of cultivated grasses are the most universally
important staple food. The range of grains and cereals covers
varieties of rice, wheat and buckwheat, corn, barley, rye,
oats, and millet, as well as their associated products
such as flour.

Grains and cereals are cheap foods which are highly nutritious,
versatile, and filling and form a good base to which other
ingredients can be added. Each has its own distinctive flavor and
texture, so experiment with lesser-known grains like millet in
Oriental-Style Millet Pilaff (see page 52) or combine a
traditional cereal like semolina with cheese to make
Cheesy Semolina Fritters (see page 50).

*Opposite: Japanese women
hanging out rice to dry after
harvesting.*

STEP 2

STEP 4

STEP 5

STEP 6

CHEESY SEMOLINA FRITTERS WITH APPLE RELISH

Based on a gnocchi recipe, these delicious fritters are accompanied by a fruity homemade relish.

SERVES 4

2½ cups milk
1 small onion
1 celery stalk
1 bay leaf
2 cloves
⅔ cup semolina
1 cup grated sharp semi-hard cheese
½ tsp dried mustard powder
2 tbsp all-purpose flour
1 egg, beaten
½ cup dried white breadcrumbs
6 tbsp vegetable oil
salt and pepper
celery leaves to garnish
coleslaw to serve

RELISH:
2 celery stalks, chopped
2 small eating apples, cored and
    diced finely
½ cup golden raisins
½ cup no-need-to-soak dried apricots,
    chopped
6 tbsp cider vinegar
pinch of ground cloves
½ tsp ground cinnamon

1 Pour the milk into a saucepan and add the onion, celery, bay leaf, and cloves. Bring to a boil, remove from the heat, and allow to stand for 15 minutes.

2 Strain into another saucepan, bring to a boil and sprinkle in the semolina, stirring constantly. Reduce the heat and simmer for 5 minutes until very thick, stirring occasionally to prevent it sticking.

3 Remove from the heat and beat in the cheese, mustard, and seasoning. Place in a greased bowl and allow to cool.

4 To make the relish, put all the ingredients in a saucepan, bring to a boil, cover, and simmer gently for 20 minutes, until tender. Allow to cool.

5 Put the flour, egg, and breadcrumbs on separate plates. Divide the cooled semolina mixture into 8 and press into 2½-in rounds, flouring the hands if necessary.

6 Coat lightly in flour, then egg and breadcrumbs. Heat the oil in a large skillet and gently fry the fritters for 3–4 minutes on each side until golden. Drain on paper towels. Garnish with celery leaves and serve with the relish and coleslaw.

STEP 1

STEP 2

STEP 3

STEP 4

ORIENTAL-STYLE MILLET PILAFF

Millet makes an interesting alternative to rice, which is the more traditional ingredient of a pilaff. Serve with a crisp salad of oriental vegetables.

SERVES 4

1¹/₂ cups millet grains
1 tbsp vegetable oil
1 bunch scallions, white and green parts, chopped
1 garlic clove, crushed
1 tsp grated ginger root
1 orange bell pepper, deseeded and diced
2¹/₂ cups water
1 orange
²/₃ cup chopped pitted dates
2 tsp sesame oil
1 cup roasted cashew nuts
2 tbsp pumpkin seeds
salt and pepper
oriental salad vegetables to serve

1 Place the millet in a large saucepan and put over a medium heat for 4–5 minutes to toast, shaking the pan occasionally until the grains begin to crack and pop.

2 Heat the oil in another saucepan and gently fry the scallions, garlic, ginger, and bell pepper for 2–3 minutes until just softened but not browned. Add the toasted millet and pour in the water.

3 Using a vegetable peeler, pare the rind from the orange and add the rind to the pan. Squeeze the juice from the orange into the pan. Season well.

4 Bring to a boil, reduce the heat, cover, and cook gently for 20 minutes until all the liquid has been absorbed. Remove from the heat, stir in the dates and sesame oil and leave to stand for 10 minutes.

5 Discard the orange rind and stir in the cashew nuts. Pile into a serving dish, sprinkle with pumpkin seeds, and serve with oriental salad vegetables.

ORANGES

For extra orange flavor, peel and segment 2 oranges and stir the segments into the mixture with the cashew nuts.

GREEN RICE

Based on the Mexican dish 'arroz verde', this recipe is perfect for bell pepper and chili lovers. Serve with iced lemonade to quell the fire!

STEP 1

RVES **4**

arge green bell peppers
resh green chilies
bsp plus 1 tsp vegetable oil
arge onion, chopped finely
arlic clove, crushed
bsp ground coriander
2 cups long-grain rice
ups Fresh Vegetable Stock (see page 76)
ups frozen peas
bsp chopped fresh cilantro
gg, beaten
t and pepper
sh cilantro to garnish

SERVE:
tilla chips
e wedges

1 Halve, core, and deseed the bell peppers. Cut the flesh into small bes. Deseed and finely chop the chilies.

2 Heat 2 tablespoons of the oil in a saucepan and gently fry the onion, rlic, bell peppers, and chilies for 5–6 nutes until softened but not browned.

3 Stir in the ground coriander, rice, and vegetable stock. Bring to a boil, ver, and simmer for 10 minutes. Add

the frozen peas, bring back to a boil, cover again, and simmer for a further 5 minutes until the rice is tender and the liquid has been absorbed. Remove from the heat and leave to stand, covered, for 10 minutes.

STEP 2

4 Season well and mix in the fresh cilantro. Pile into a warmed serving dish and keep warm.

5 Heat the remaining oil in a small omelet pan, pour in the egg, and cook for 1–2 minutes on each side until set. Slide onto a plate, roll up, and slice into thin rounds.

6 Arrange the omelet strips on top of the rice. Garnish with cilantro and serve with tortilla chips and lime wedges.

STEP 3

CHILIES

Be careful not to touch your face, particularly your eyes, when preparing chilies as the juice can be an irritant. Wash your hands immediately after or wear rubber gloves.

STEP 5

STEP 1

STEP 2

STEP 4

STEP 5

COUSCOUS ROYALE

*Serve this stunning dish as a centerpiece for a Moroccan-style feast;
a truly memorable meal.*

SERVES 6

3 carrots
3 zucchini
12 oz pumpkin or squash
5 cups Fresh Vegetable Stock (see page 76)
2 cinnamon sticks, broken in half
2 tsp ground cumin
1 tsp ground coriander
pinch of saffron strands
2 tbsp olive oil
pared rind and juice of 1 lemon
2 tbsp clear honey
2²/₃ cups pre-cooked couscous
¼ cup butter or margarine, softened
1 cup large seedless raisins
salt and pepper
fresh cilantro to garnish

1 Cut the carrots and zucchini into 3-in. pieces and cut in half lengthwise.

2 Trim the pumpkin or squash and discard the seeds. Peel and cut into pieces the same size as the carrots and zucchini.

3 Put the stock, spices, saffron, and carrots in a large saucepan. Bring to a boil, skim off any scum, and add the olive oil. Simmer for 15 minutes.

4 Add the lemon rind and juice to the pan with the honey, zucchini, and pumpkin or squash. Season well. Bring back to a boil and simmer for a further 10 minutes.

5 Meanwhile, soak the couscous according to the packet instructions. Transfer to a steamer or large strainer lined with cheesecloth and place over the vegetable pan. Cover and steam as directed. Stir in the butter or margarine.

6 Pile the couscous onto a warmed serving plate. Drain the vegetables, reserving the stock, lemon rind, and cinnamon. Arrange the vegetables on top of the couscous. Put the raisins on top and spoon over 6 tablespoons of the reserved stock. Keep warm.

7 Return the remaining stock to the heat and boil for 5 minutes to reduce slightly. Discard the lemon rind and cinnamon. Garnish with the cilantro and serve with the sauce handed separately.

STEP 1

STEP 2

STEP 3

STEP 4

INDONESIAN HOT RICE SALAD

Nutty brown rice combines well with peanuts and a sweet and sour mixture of fruit and vegetables in this tangy combination.

SERVES 4

1½ cups brown rice
14-oz can pineapple pieces in natural juice, drained
1 bunch scallions, chopped
1 red bell pepper, deseeded and chopped
2 cups beansprouts
¾ cup dry-roasted peanuts
4 oz radishes, sliced thinly

DRESSING:
2 tbsp crunchy peanut butter
1 tbsp groundnut oil
2 tbsp light soy sauce
2 tbsp white wine vinegar
2 tsp clear honey
1 tsp chili powder
½ tsp garlic salt
pepper

1 Place the rice in a saucepan and cover with water. Bring to a boil, cover, and simmer for 30 minutes until tender.

2 Meanwhile, make the dressing. Place all the ingredients in a small bowl and beat for a few seconds until well combined.

3 Drain the rice and place in a heatproof bowl. Heat the dressing in a small saucepan for 1 minute and then toss into the rice and mix well.

4 Working quickly, stir in the pineapple, scallions, bell pepper, beansprouts, and peanuts.

5 Pile into a warmed serving bowl or dish, arrange the radish slices around the outside, and serve immediately.

SERVING COLD

This salad is equally delicious served cold. Add the dressing to the rice while still warm, but allow the rice to cool before adding the remaining ingredients.

STEP 2

STEP 3

STEP 4

STEP 5

PESTO RICE WITH GARLIC BREAD

Try this combination of two types of rice with the richness of pine nuts, basil, and Parmesan cheese, and accompanied by an irresistible garlic-soaked bread.

SERVES 4

*1½ cups mixed long-grain and wild rice
sprigs of fresh basil to garnish
tomato and orange salad to serve*

*PESTO DRESSING:
½ oz fresh basil
1 cup pine nuts
2 garlic cloves, crushed
6 tbsp olive oil
½ cup grated Parmesan cheese
salt and pepper*

*GARLIC BREAD:
2 small Granary or wholegrain sticks of
   French bread
⅓ cup butter or margarine, softened
2 garlic cloves, crushed
1 tsp dried mixed herbs*

1 Place the rice in a saucepan and cover with water. Bring to a boil and cook according to the packet instructions. Drain well and keep warm.

2 Meanwhile, make the pesto dressing. Remove the basil leaves from the stalks and finely chop the leaves. Reserve ¼ cup of the pine nuts and finely chop the remainder. Mix with the chopped basil and dressing

ingredients. Alternatively, put all the ingredients in a food processor or blende and blend for a few seconds until smooth Set aside.

3 To make the garlic bread, slice the bread at 1-in. intervals, taking car not to slice all the way through. Mix the butter or margarine with the garlic, herbs, and seasoning. Spread thickly between each slice.

4 Wrap the bread in foil and bake in a preheated oven at 400°F for 10–15 minutes.

5 To serve, toast the reserved pine nuts under a preheated medium broiler for 2–3 minutes until golden. To the pesto dressing into the hot rice and pile into a warmed serving dish. Sprinkl with toasted pine nuts and garnish with basil sprigs. Serve with the garlic bread and a tomato and orange salad.

CHAPTER FIVE

Pastries & Pancakes

pular with so many people, pastry dishes can be served either for mple suppers, such as Green Vegetable Gougère (see page 74) or, like White Nut Filo Parcels (see page 73), for more elaborate, pecial-occasion meals. If you haven't the time to make your own stry, most shops sell good fresh and frozen ready-made pie dough, whole wheat, puff, and filo pastries.

Pancakes are known the world over in different forms. Egg and ilk-based recipes are well known in Europe and use white, whole heat or buckwheat flours, whereas white flour and water-based ancakes are more familiar in India, China, and Central America; the tortillas of Mexico, for example, which are used in delicious dishes such as Chili Bean Curd Enchilladas (see page 68).

Opposite: Made from a few simple store-cupboard ingredients, pancakes make a convenient, versatile dish that's always popular.

STEP 2

STEP 3

STEP 6

STEP 7

MEDITERRANEAN VEGETABLE TART

A rich tomato pastry base topped with a mouthwatering selection of vegetables and cheese makes a tart that's tasty as well as attractive.

SERVES 6

1 eggplant, sliced
2 tbsp salt
4 tbsp olive oil
1 garlic clove, crushed
1 large yellow bell pepper, sliced
1¼ cups ready-made tomato pasta sauce
⅔ cup sun-dried tomatoes in oil, drained and
    halved if necessary
6 oz Mozzarella cheese, drained and sliced
    thinly

DOUGH:
2 cups all-purpose flour
pinch of celery salt
½ cup butter or margarine
2 tbsp tomato paste
2–3 tbsp milk

1 To make the dough, sift the flour and celery salt into a bowl and rub in the butter or margarine until the mixture resembles breadcrumbs.

2 Mix together the tomato paste and milk and stir into the mixture to form a firm dough. Knead gently on a lightly floured surface until smooth. Wrap and chill for 30 minutes.

3 Grease an 11 inch loose-bottomed flan pan. Roll out the dough on a lightly floured surface and use to line the pan. Trim and prick all over with a fork. Chill for 30 minutes.

4 Meanwhile, layer the eggplant in a dish, sprinkling with the salt. Leave for 30 minutes.

5 Bake the dough case in a preheated oven at 400°F for 20–25 minutes until cooked and lightly golden. Set aside. Increase the oven temperature to 450°.

6 Rinse the eggplant and pat dry. Heat 3 tablespoons of the oil in a skillet and gently fry the garlic, eggplant, and bell pepper for 5–6 minutes until just softened. Drain on paper towels.

7 Spread the pastry case with pasta sauce and arrange the cooked vegetables, sun-dried tomatoes, and Mozzarella on top. Brush with the remaining oil and bake for 5 minutes until the cheese is just melting. Serve.

STEP 2

STEP 5

STEP 6

STEP 7

SPINACH PANCAKE LAYER

Nutty-tasting buckwheat pancakes are combined with a cheesy spinach mixture and baked with a crispy topping.

SERVES 4

1 cup buckwheat flour
1 egg, beaten
1 tbsp walnut oil
1¼ cups milk
2 tsp vegetable oil

FILLING:
2 lb young spinach leaves
2 tbsp water
1 bunch scallions, white and green parts,
    chopped
2 tsp walnut oil
1 egg, beaten
1 egg yolk
1 cup cottage cheese
½ tsp grated nutmeg
¼ cup grated semi-hard cheese
¼ cup walnut pieces
salt and pepper

1 Sift the flour into a bowl and add any husks that remain behind in the strainer.

2 Make a well in the center and add the egg and walnut oil. Gradually beat in the milk to make a smooth batter. Leave to stand for 30 minutes.

3 To make the filling, wash the spinach and pack into a saucepan with the water. Cover tightly and cook on a high heat for 5–6 minutes until soft.

4 Drain well and leave to cool. Gently fry the scallions in the walnut oil for 2–3 minutes until just soft. Drain on paper towels. Set aside.

5 Beat the batter. Brush a small crêpe pan with oil, heat until hot, and pour in enough batter to lightly cover the base. Cook for 1–2 minutes until set, turn, and cook for 1 minute until golden. Turn onto a warmed plate. Repeat to make 8–10 pancakes, layering them with baking parchment.

6 Chop the spinach and dry with paper towels. Mix with the scallions, egg, egg yolk, cottage cheese, nutmeg, and seasoning.

7 Layer the pancakes and spinach mixture on a cookie sheet lined with baking parchment, finishing with a pancake. Sprinkle with the grated cheese and bake in a preheated oven at 375°F for 20–25 minutes until firm and golden. Sprinkle with walnuts and serve.

STEP 1

STEP 4

STEP 5

STEP 6

CHILI BEAN CURD ENCHILLADAS

A tasty Mexican-style dish with a melt-in-the-mouth combination of bean curd and avocado served with a tangy tomato sauce.

SERVES 4

$1/2$ tsp chili powder
1 tsp paprika
2 tbsp all-purpose flour
8 oz bean curd, cut into $1/2$ inch pieces
2 tbsp vegetable oil
1 onion, chopped finely
1 garlic clove, crushed
1 large red bell pepper, deseeded and chopped
   finely
1 large ripe avocado
1 tbsp lime juice
4 tomatoes, peeled, deseeded and chopped
1 cup grated semi-hard cheese
8 soft flour tortillas
$2/3$ cup sour cream
salt and pepper
sprigs of fresh cilantro to garnish
pickled green jalapeño chilies to serve

SAUCE:
$3 1/2$ cups sugocasa (see page 10)
3 tbsp chopped fresh parsley
3 tbsp chopped fresh cilantro

1 Mix the chili powder, paprika, flour, and seasoning on a plate and coat the bean curd pieces.

2 Heat the oil in a skillet and gently fry the bean curd for 3–4 minutes

until golden. Remove with a perforated spoon, drain on paper towels and set aside.

3 Add the onion, garlic, and bell pepper to the oil and gently fry for 2–3 minutes until just softened. Drain and set aside.

4 Halve the avocado, peel, and remove the pit. Slice lengthwise, put in a bowl with the lime juice, and to to coat.

5 Add the bean curd and onion mixture and gently mix in the tomatoes and half the cheese. Spoon the filling down the center of each tortilla, top with sour cream and roll up. Put in a shallow ovenproof dish.

6 To make the sauce, mix together all the ingredients. Spoon over the tortillas, sprinkle with the remaining cheese, and bake in a preheated oven at 375°F for 25 minutes until golden and bubbling. Garnish with cilantro and serve with jalapeño chilies.

STEP 2

STEP 3

STEP 4

STEP 6

CREAMY MUSHROOM
VOL-AU-VENT

A simple mixture of creamy, tender mushrooms filling a crisp, rich pastry case, this dish will make an impression at any dinner party.

SERVES 4

1 lb puff pastry, thawed if frozen
1 egg, beaten, for glazing

FILLING:
2 tbsp butter or margarine
1½ lb mixed mushrooms such as open cup, field, button, chestnut, shiitake, pied de mouton, sliced
6 tbsp dry white wine
4 tbsp heavy cream
2 tbsp chopped fresh chervil
salt and pepper
sprigs of fresh chervil to garnish

1 Roll out the pastry dough on a lightly floured surface to an 8 inch square.

2 Using a sharp knife, mark a square 1 inch from the dough edge, cutting halfway through the dough.

3 Score the top in a diagonal pattern. Knock up the edges with a kitchen knife and put on a cookie sheet. Brush the top with beaten egg, taking care not to let the egg run into the cut. Bake in a preheated oven at 425°F for 35 minutes.

4 Cut out the central square. Discard the soft pastry inside the case, leaving the base intact. Return to the oven, with the square, for 10 minutes.

5 Meanwhile, make the filling. Melt the butter or margarine in a skillet and stir-fry the mushrooms over a high heat for 3 minutes.

6 Add the wine and cook for 10 minutes, stirring occasionally, until the mushrooms have softened. Stir in the cream, chervil, and seasoning. Pile into the pastry case. Top with the pastry square, garnish, and serve.

MUSHROOMS

Choose mushrooms that smell fresh and fragrant; avoid bruised or brownish ones. Store for 24–36 hours in the refrigerator, in paper bags, as they 'sweat' in plastic.

There's no need to peel mushrooms. Wild mushrooms should be washed carefully, but other cultivated varieties are better simply wiped with paper towels.

WHITE NUT FILO PARCELS

hese crisp, buttery parcels, filled with nuts and pesto, would make an
interesting break with tradition for Sunday lunch, or even as part of
your Thanksgiving meal.

STEP 2

RVES **4**

bsp butter or margarine
arge onion, chopped finely
cups mixed white nuts, such as pine
uts, unsalted cashew nuts, blanched
lmonds, unsalted peanuts, chopped
inely
cups fresh white breadcrumbs
tsp ground mace
gg, beaten
gg yolk
bsp pesto sauce
bsp chopped fresh basil
cup melted butter or margarine
sheets filo pastry
t and pepper
igs of fresh basil to garnish

SERVE:
nberry sauce
amed vegetables

Melt the butter or margarine in a
skillet and gently fry the onion for
3 minutes until just softened but not
owned.

Remove from the heat and stir in
the nuts, 1 cup of the breadcrumbs,
mace, seasoning, and beaten egg. Set
de.

3 Place the remaining breadcrumbs
in a bowl and stir in the egg yolk,
pesto sauce, basil, and 1 tablespoon of
the melted butter or margarine. Mix well.

4 Brush 1 sheet of filo with melted
butter or margarine. Fold in half
and brush again. Repeat with a second
sheet and lay on top of the first one to
form a cross.

5 Divide the nut mixture and pesto
mixture into 8 portions each. Put a
portion of nut mixture in the center of
the pastry. Top with a portion of the
pesto mixture. Fold over the edges,
brushing with more butter or margarine,
to form a parcel. Brush the top with
butter or margarine and transfer to a
cookie sheet.

6 Continue with the remaining
pastry and fillings to make 8
parcels. Brush with the remaining butter
or margarine and bake in a preheated
oven at 425°F for 15–20 minutes until
golden. Garnish with basil sprigs and
serve with cranberry sauce and steamed
vegetables.

STEP 3

STEP 4

STEP 5

STEP 2

STEP 3

STEP 4

STEP 6

GREEN VEGETABLE GOUGERE

A tasty, simple supper dish of choux pastry and crisp green vegetables. The choux pastry ring can be filled with all kinds of vegetables, so try experimenting with your own favorites.

SERVES 6

1¼ cups all-purpose flour
½ cup butter or margarine
1¼ cups water
4 eggs, beaten
¾ cup grated Swiss cheese
1 tbsp milk
salt and pepper

FILLING:
2 tbsp garlic and herb butter or
  margarine
2 tsp olive oil
2 leeks, shredded
8 oz green cabbage, shredded finely
4 oz beansprouts
½ tsp grated lime rind
1 tbsp lime juice
celery salt and pepper
lime slices to garnish

1 Sift the flour onto a piece of baking parchment and set aside. Cut the butter or margarine into dice and put in a saucepan with the water. Heat until the butter has melted.

2 Bring the butter and water to a boil, then shoot in the flour all at once. Beat until the mixture becomes thick. Remove from the heat and beat until the mixture is glossy and comes away from the sides of the saucepan.

3 Transfer to a mixing bowl and cool for 10 minutes. Gradually beat in the eggs, a little at a time, making sure they are thoroughly incorporated after each addition. Stir in ½ cup of the cheese and season.

4 Dampen a cookie sheet. Place spoonfuls of the mixture in a 9 inch round on the cookie sheet. Brush with milk and sprinkle with the remaining cheese. Bake in a preheated oven at 425°F for 30–35 minutes until golden and crisp. Transfer to a warmed serving plate.

5 Make the filling about 5 minutes before the end of cooking time. Heat the butter or margarine and the oil in a large skillet and stir-fry the leeks and cabbage for 2 minutes.

6 Add the beansprouts, lime rind, and lime juice and cook for 1 minute, stirring. Season and pile into the center of the cooked pastry ring. Garnish with lime slices and serve.

THE VEGETARIAN DIET

FRESH VEGETABLE STOCK

This stock can be kept chilled for up to 3 days or frozen for up to 3 months. Salt is not added when cooking the stock; it is better to season it according to the dish it is to be used in.

MAKES 1½ QUARTS

8 oz shallots
1 large carrot, diced
1 celery stalk, chopped
½ fennel bulb
1 garlic clove
1 bay leaf
a few fresh parsley and tarragon
    sprigs
2 quarts water
pepper

1. Put all the ingredients in a large saucepan and bring to a boil.
2. Skim off surface scum with a flat spoon. Reduce to a gentle simmer, partially cover, and cook for 45 minutes. Leave to cool.
3. Line a strainer with clean cheesecloth and put over a large pitcher or bowl. Pour the stock through the strainer. Discard the herbs and vegetables. Cover and store in the refrigerator for up to 3 days or freeze in small quantities.

Vegetarianism is becoming increasingly popular in the West. Some people choose not to eat meat because of their feelings about animal cruelty, while others believe that cutting out meat will help reduce the risk of heart disease caused by eating cholesterol-rich foods, and that eating more fibrous vegetables and pulses will help reduce the risk of cancers such as colonic cancer. Whatever your reason for eating meals without meat, providing your meals are properly planned and varied, a vegetarian diet can be as interesting as it is healthy.

VEGETARIAN NUTRITION
When following a vegetarian diet, your food intake must be carefully thought out in order to ensure the diet is well balanced and provides the body with the correct nourishment. The use of milk, cheese, eggs, pulses, and cereals should be maximized to provide sufficient protein, vitamins, and minerals. Resist the temptation to eat large amounts of dairy produce in place of meat, however, as cream, butter, and cheese contain cholesterol and a lot of fat. As with any diet, keep everything in moderation.

Proteins
Protein is made up of smaller units, called amino acids, which combine to help the body with growth, repair, maintenance, and protection.

   There are eight essential amino acids; some foods are better at providing these than others. The main sources of protein for vegetarians are dairy produce (which contains all the essential amino acids), and nuts and seeds, pulses, cereals and cereal products, each of which is deficie in at least one amino acid. Because of this, two or more of these sources must be eaten at the same meal or combined with dairy produce if they are to be of value to the body.

Carbohydrates
Used by the body for energy, the two main groups of carbohydrates are starches and sugars, which are present cereals and grains and related products such as flour. They are also found in fruits, pulses, and some vegetables.

Sugar: Whether white, brown, or in the form of honey, syrup, or molasses, suga is purely a source of energy and has no other nutritional value. Use any type of sugar in moderation and avoid excessiv intake.

Dietary fiber: Many carbohydrates in their natural, unrefined form, such as whole wheat flour, contain dietary fiber It does not have any nutritional value but is vital for the efficient working of th digestive system and the elimination of waste matter. Some types of fiber may also slow down the rate at which the body absorbs carbohydrates. A vegetarian diet is naturally high in fiber There is no fiber in meat, poultry, fish, o dairy produce. Good sources of fiber are pulses, whole grains, vegetables

ecially corn, spinach, and baked
atoes), dried fruits, and fresh fruits.
to include at least one high-fiber food
meal.

s
most concentrated form of energy in
diet and a vital carrier of vitamins A
D. Fat comes in two forms: animal
vegetable. The only animal fats in
vegetarian diet are found in dairy
duce and egg yolks.
ats can be classified as saturated,
nounsaturated, and polyunsaturated.
urated fats, such as butter, are solid at
m temperature and are believed to
e the quantity of fat and cholesterol in
blood; monounsaturated fats, such as
e oil, are thought to decrease the risk
eart disease and may lower blood
ssure; polyunsaturated fats, such as
flower and corn oils, were at one time
eved to be better than mono-
saturated fats at lowering the amount
holesterol in the blood, but latest
earch has found no difference between
two. Polyunsaturated margarines
fats are an exception, however. The
are made solid by a process called
lrogenation and it is thought that this
cess can make the fats more harmful
n saturated fats. It is important to be
are of this when choosing an
rnative to butter. Whatever you
oose, keep your intake of fat to a
sible level and cut down wherever
sible. Always read nutritional labeling
'hidden' fats.

Vitamins and minerals

Vegetables are lower in certain vitamins
and minerals than animal products, so it
is essential to plan your food intake to
obtain the correct nutritional balance.

Vitamin B group: Important for the
metabolism of other foods, the health of
the nervous system, and the production
of red blood cells. You will obtain a good
supply by eating grains, cereals, leafy
green vegetables, nuts and seeds, and
dried fruits. Yeast extract, wheatgerm,
and brewer's yeast are also good sources.

There are three B vitamins which
vegetarians may lack if they consume
little or no dairy produce: vitamin B2
(riboflavin), vitamin B3 (nicotinic acid),
and vitamin B12. Good sources of
vitamins B2 and B3 are mushrooms,
sesame seeds, sunflower seeds, almonds,
prunes, and dried peaches. Vitamin B12
is found mainly in animal products and
supplementation is often advised for
vegans, as deficiency can lead to anemia
and nerve damage. Yeast extract, alfalfa
sprouts, seaweed, textured vegetable
proteins, and fortified soya milk are
other sources of vitamin B12.

Calcium: Essential for bone and teeth
formation, and for the functioning of
nerves and muscles. The best sources are
dairy produce and eggs. Vegans and
those who don't eat many dairy foods
need to eat more grains, pulses, nuts,
seeds, and dried fruits to obtain a good
supply of calcium.

BECHAMEL SAUCE

This basic white sauce can be
use in all kinds of dishes: flavor
it with grated cheese or
chopped fresh herbs, if you like.

MAKES 2½ CUPS

2½ cups milk
4 cloves
1 bay leaf
pinch of grated nutmeg
2 tbsp butter or margarine
¼ cup all-purpose flour
salt and pepper

1. Put the milk in a saucepan
and add the cloves, bay leaf,
and nutmeg. Gradually bring
to a boil, remove from the heat,
and leave for 15 minutes.
2. Melt the butter or margarine
in another saucepan and stir in
the flour to form a roux. Cook,
stirring, for 1 minute. Remove
from the heat. Strain the milk
and gradually blend into the
roux.
3. Return to the heat and bring
to a boil, stirring, until the
sauce thickens. Simmer gently
for 2–3 minutes. Season and
add any flavorings.

TAHINI CREAM

Tahini is a paste made from sesame seeds. This nutty flavored sauce is good served with Kofta Kebabs (see page 24), and other Middle Eastern dishes such as falafel.

3 tbsp tahini
6 tbsp water
2 tsp lemon juice
1 garlic clove, crushed
salt and pepper

Blend together the tahini and water. Stir in the lemon juice and garlic, season, and serve.

Iron: Lack of iron can lead to anemia as it is essential for the production of red blood cells which carry oxygen around the body. Eggs are an excellent source, as are dark green leafy vegetables, broccoli, dried apricots and figs, pulses, and nuts. However, as iron from vegetable sources is not readily absorbed by the body, it is important to eat foods rich in vitamin C at the same meal as this aids the absorption of iron.

Zinc: An important trace element for growth, healing, reproduction, and the digestion of protein and carbohydrate. Although wholegrains and pulses contain zinc, a substance called phytic acid inhibits its absorption. Other sources are wheatgerm, oats, nuts, and seeds. Useful amounts can be found in most yellow and green vegetables and fruits.

VEGETARIAN INGREDIENTS

At the heart of any balanced diet is an interesting variety of ingredients.

Nuts and seeds

Nuts and seeds provide valuable quantities of protein, B vitamins, iron, and calcium but also have a high fat content. Nuts and seeds are often pressed for their oil or made into pastes and butters. They add a wealth of flavors to dishes as well as adding texture.

Pulses

High in fiber and protein and low in fat, beans, peas, and lentils are found in all sizes and colors. They are cheap to buy their dry form, but most require overnight soaking before boiling. If you are short of time, use canned pulses. Although canned pulses are more expensive, they are ready cooked and ready to use. Choose varieties that are canned in water without added sugar and salt. Always drain canned pulses a rinse well in cold water before use.

Grains and cereals

Very important components of the vegetarian diet, supplying fiber, carbohydrates, protein, iron, zinc, calcium, and B vitamins. Grains and cereals bulk out the diet and add texture

Pasta

A high carbohydrate food which, like grains and cereals, forms the basis of th vegetarian diet. Made from white, whol wheat or rice flour. All types of fresh pasta, and some dried varieties, contain egg.

Vegetables

These can be categorized into different groups:
Leaves: Lettuces, spinach, watercress, chard, vine leaves. Contain calcium, iron, and fiber.
Brassicas: Cabbage, broccoli, kale, Brussels sprouts, cauliflower, Chinese leaves. Rich in vitamins and minerals.
Pods and seeds: Fresh beans, corn, peas snow peas, okra. Full of fiber and a good source of protein.

ots: Asparagus, celery, endive,
nboo, artichoke, fennel. Better known
flavor, texture, and shape than
ritional value.

bs: Onions, garlic, leeks, shallots.
ellent for flavor.

ts: Celery root, carrots, turnips,
abaga, beet, mooli. Contain iron,
cium, and protein. Carrots are also
y rich in vitamin A.

ers: White and sweet potatoes, yams,
salem artichokes. High in
bohydrate, and useful sources of
min C, iron, and protein.

uits': Tomatoes, avocado, bell peppers,
lies, eggplant. Rich in vitamin C.

cumbers and squash: Including
chini, pumpkins and squash. Very
h water content, Contain some fiber.

shrooms: Rich in vitamins B2 and B3.

vegetables: Increasingly popular and
y nutritious. Rich in protein, iron,
cium, and vitamin B12.

uits

m home-grown varieties such as
les, pears, and soft fruits, to the more
tic imports such as lychees, mangoes,
pineapples, fruits are a valuable
rce of vitamin C and fiber as well as
cific trace elements: bananas, for
mple, are an excellent source of
gnesium and vitamin B6, and
ngoes provide zinc.

ried fruits are higher in fiber and B
mins and have a richer flavor than
h fruit. Look out for sun-dried fruits,
those free from sulfur dioxide, which

is used to prevent darkening during
drying. Sulfur dioxide inhibits the
absorption of vitamin B1 in the body. To
cut down on its effect, wash dried fruit in
warm water, boil for 5 minutes, then
rinse again.

Dairy and non-dairy products

Cheeses, eggs, milk, yogurt, creams, and
bean curd are valuable sources of
protein, calcium, vitamins A and D, and
iron. Cheese adds an excellent flavor to
many dishes. Many varieties of
vegetarian cheeses, which are made
using non-animal rennet, are available.
If you choose not to eat dairy products,
check the nutritional content of non-
dairy products, such as soya milks, and
look out for fortified varieties. Bean curd
is made from soya milk and is available in
many forms – firm, soft, dried, or smoked.
It is low in fat and high in protein. It is
very versatile and can be fried or added to
casseroles and soups. It has a neutral
flavor and absorbs flavors from the foods
it is cooked with.

Herbs and spices

Careful combining of fresh or dried herbs
and spices can add extra zest and flavor
to any dish: they help stimulate the taste
buds and aid digestion. Experiment with
different flavors and read the packet if
you are uncertain about strength – most
show possible uses and suggested
quantities. Don't let any one flavor
dominate, they should blend to form a
perfect balance.

SALAD DRESSINGS

Salads are the tastiest and most
nutritious way to eat many
vegetables. This refreshing,
chilled dressing and rich, warm
one will liven up all kinds of
salads and vegetables.

Cucumber Dressing

scant 1 cup natural yogurt
2 inch piece cucumber, peeled
1 tbsp chopped fresh mint leaves
1/2 tsp grated lemon rind
pinch of superfine sugar
salt and pepper

Put the ingredients in a blender
or food processor and process
until smooth. Alternatively,
finely chop the cucumber and
combine with the other
ingredients. Serve chilled.

Warm Walnut Dressing

6 tbsp walnut oil
3 tbsp white wine vinegar
1 tbsp clear honey
1 tsp wholegrain mustard
1 garlic clove, sliced
salt and pepper

Put the oil, vinegar, honey,
mustard, and seasoning in a
saucepan and beat together.
Add the garlic and heat very
gently for 3 minutes. Remove
the garlic slices with a
perforated spoon and discard.
Pour the dressing over the
salad and serve immediately.

INDEX